# The Little Book of Horse Quotes

ISBN 10: 0983918260
ISBN 13: 9780983918264

Library of Congress Control Number: 2013939488
Little Quote Books
Chicago, Illinois


www.littlequotebooks.com

# The Little Book of Horse Quotes

Edited by Gina Pecho & Jessica Pecho

Illinois Horse Rescue of Will County

Illinois Horse Rescue
OF WILL COUNTY

# Table of Contents

# *Thank You*

We are so thankful for the support we receive each year from both donations and our volunteers. Our organization is run solely on donations from the kind and generous people who care about the animals we save. Our staff is made up entirely of volunteers. This allows all donations to directly benefit our horses!

Thanks above all to the rescue horses—who have shown us time and again that they have a bigger purpose in life. They are the "super stars" that now have a chance to shine their light on the lives of both children and adults in our community.

# Introduction

This is a collection of 365 quotes—a quote to use as inspiration for each day of the year. Quotes have been selected to cover a dozen topics. They are arranged for easy access as follows:

* Caring
* Companionship
* Compassion
* Giving
* Healing
* Kindness
* Laughter
* Love
* Respect
* Rewarding
* Understanding
* Uplifting

The quotes are arranged alphabetically by author in each chapter so that you can easily find your favorite quotes by author and by topic.

These quotes have been selected from around the world— from famous quotes and quotes from horse lovers, cowboys, and cowgirls to savvy sayings and uplifting proverbs. This collection is organized with lots of horse sense in mind to share the laughter, love, and lessons that horses bring into our daily lives each and every day of the year. May these quotes shine a light in your heart as our rescue horses do for us. We hope that you enjoy this book of our favorite horse quotes.

See you in the barn!

Gina Pecho and Jessica Pecho
Illinois Horse Rescue of Will County

August 2013

# Caring

No hour of *life* spent in the saddle is WASTED

Always be humble enough to learn something new.
Otherwise, it's only a matter of time before your
knowledge becomes outdated.

~ *Clinton Anderson*

Many people have sighed for the "good old days" and
regretted the "passing of the horse," but today, when
only those who like horses own them, it is a far better
time for horses.

~ *C.W. Anderson*

A horse can lend its rider the speed and strength he or
she lacks, but the rider who is wise remembers it is no
more than a loan.

~ *Pam Brown*

God forbid that I should go to any heaven in which there are no horses.

~ *Robert Browning*

A thousand horse and none to ride!
With flowing tail, and flying mane,
Wide nostrils never stretched by pain,
Mouths bloodless to the bit or rein,
And feet that iron never shod,
And flanks unscarred by spur or rod,
A thousand horse, the wild, the free,
Like waves that follow o'er the sea,
Came thickly thundering on,...

~ *Lord Byron*

No hour of life is wasted that is spent in the saddle.

~ *Winston Churchill*

Live each day with courage.
Take pride in your work.
Always finish what you start.
Do what has to be done.
Be tough, but fair.
When you make a promise, keep it.
Ride for the brand.
Talk less and say more.
Remember that some things aren't for sale.
Know where to draw the line.

*~ Code of the West*

Show me your horse and I will tell you who you are.

*~ Jane Crowley*

In training horses, one trains himself.

*~ Antoine De Pluvinet*

A horse which stops dead just before a jump and thus propels its rider into a graceful arc provides a splendid excuse for general merriment.

~ *Duke of Edinburgh*

Do not go where the path may lead, go instead where there is no path and leave a trail.

~ *Ralph Waldo Emerson*

A horse is uncomfortable in the middle and dangerous at both ends.

~ *Ian Fleming*

To me, horses and freedom are synonymous.

~ *Veryl Goodnight*

The horse knows. He knows if you know. He also knows if you don't know.

~ *Ray Hunt*

The horse through all its trials has preserved the sweetness of paradise in its blood.

~ *Johannes Jensen*

Nobody ever drowned in his own sweat.

~ *Ann Landers*

Don't change horses while crossing a stream.

~ *Abraham Lincoln*

A horse doesn't care how much you know, until he knows how much you care.

~ *Pat Parelli*

Small children are convinced that ponies deserve to see the inside of the house.

*~ Maya Patel*

Horses and children, I often think, have a lot of the good sense there is in the world.

*~ Josephine Demott Robinson*

Spending that many hours in the saddle gave a man plenty of time to think. That's why so many cowboys fancied themselves Philosophers.

*~ Charles M. Russell*

People have always cared me a bit, you see—they're so complicated. I suppose that's why I prefer horses.

**~ From the movie *Separate Tables*, 1958**

...there's nothin' in life that's worth doin', if it cain't
be done from a horse....

~ *Red Steagall*

There is just as much horse sense as ever, but the
horses have most of it.

~ *Author Unknown*

A cowboy's hands are as strong as steel as tough as
leather put soft enough to touch a hummingbirds
wing and the skin of a woman and not disturb the
beauty of either.

~ *Cowboy Wisdom*

Shirts that cost more than a week's worth of groceries
are like horseshoes that cost more than a horse.

~ *Cowboy Wisdom*

Ain't worth fussin' about unless the bone is showin'
or you ain't got no feelin' in it...even then you should
cowboy up and walk it off.

~ *Cowboy Wisdom*

A real cowboy doesn't have to say they are a cowboy you know, the smell, the expression and the heart tells itself.

~ *Cowboy Wisdom*

"Cowgirl Up" means to rise to the occasion, not to give up, and to do it all without whining or complaining.

~ *Cowgirl Wisdom*

Cowgirls aren't made, they are born.

~ *Cowgirl Wisdom*

It ain't the clothes that make the cowgirl, it's the attitude and heart.

~ *Cowgirl Wisdom*

# Companionship

A pony is a childhood dream, a horse is an adulthood treasure

Rebecca Carroll.

When riding a horse we leave our fear, troubles, and
sadness behind on the ground.

~ *Juli Carlson*

A pony is a childhood dream; a horse is an adult
treasure.

~ *Rebecca Carroll*

Riding a horse is not a gentle hobby, to be picked up
and laid down like a game of Solitaire. It is a grand
passion.

~ *Ralph Waldo Emerson*

The essential joy of being with horses is that it brings us in contact with the rare elements of grace, beauty, spirit, and fire.

~ *Sharon Ralls Lemon*

A lovely horse is always an experience....It is an emotional experience of the kind that is spoiled by words.

~ *Beryl Markham*

O! for a horse with wings!

~ *William Shakespeare*

In riding a horse we borrow freedom.

~ *Helen Thomson*

To ride a horse is to ride the sky.

~ *Author Unknown*

As you grow up you realize it's less important to have more friends and more important to have real ones.

*~ Author Unknown*


A best friend can see you walk in with a smile on your face and still know something's wrong.

*~ Author Unknown*


In my opinion, a horse is the animal to have. Eleven-hundred pounds of raw muscle, power, grace, and sweat between your legs—it's something you just can't get from a pet hamster.

*~ Author Unknown*


If you want a stable friendship, get a horse.

*~ Author Unknown*


In the quiet light of the stable, you hear a muffled snort, a stamp of a hoof, a friendly nicker. Gentle eyes inquire "How are you old friend?" and suddenly, all your troubles fade away.

*~ Author Unknown*


Friends leave when life is boring and boyfriends leave when times are tough, but a horse will always be with you.

*~ Author Unknown*

A stubborn horse walks behind you, an impatient horse walks in front of you, but a noble companion walks beside you.

*~ Author Unknown*

If you get to thinkin' you're a person of some influence, try orderin' somebody else's dog around.

*~ Cowboy Wisdom*

Don't worry about bitin' off more'n you can chew; your mouth is probably a whole lot bigger'n you think.

*~ Cowboy Wisdom*

Always drink upstream from the herd.

*~ Cowboy Wisdom*

Never ask a barber if you need a haircut.

*~ Cowboy Wisdom*

Generally, you ain't learnin' nothing when your mouth's a-jawin'.

*~ Cowboy Wisdom*

Good judgment comes from experience, and a lotta that comes from bad judgment.

*~ Cowboy Wisdom*


When you give a personal lesson in meanness to a critter or to a person, don't be surprised if they learn their lesson.

*~ Cowboy Wisdom*


When you're throwin' your weight around, be ready to have it thrown around by somebody else.

*~ Cowboy Wisdom*


Lettin' the cat outta the bag is a whole lot easier than puttin' it back.

*~ Cowboy Wisdom*


You can't tell how good a man or a watermelon is 'til they get thumped.

*~ Cowboy Wisdom*


Never miss a good chance to shut up.

*~ Cowboy Wisdom*

If you find yourself in a hole, the first thing to do is stop diggin'.

~ *Cowboy Wisdom*

If it don't seem like it's worth the effort, it probably ain't.

~ *Cowboy Wisdom*

# Compassion

Let your Horse
teach you about
yourself,
for you may be
at the age
where no one
else can

Heaven is high and earth wide. If you ride three feet higher above the ground than other men, you will know what that means.

~ *Rudolf C. Binding*

The horse needs to respect you, but sometimes people confuse respect and fear. And they're not the same at all.

~ *Buck Brannaman*

People ought to quit worrying so much about whispering to their horses and just start listening to them.

~ *Greg Darnall*

When I hear somebody talk about a horse or a cow
being stupid, I figure it's a sure sign that animal has
outfoxed them.

*~ Tom Dorance*

Where in this wide world can man find nobility
without pride,
Friendship without envy,
Or beauty without vanity?
Here, where grace is served with muscle
And strength by gentleness confined
He serves without servility; he has fought without
enmity.
There is nothing so powerful, nothing less violent.
There is nothing so quick, nothing more patient.

*~ Ronald Duncan*

The greatness of a nation and its moral progress can be
judged by the way its animals are treated.

*~ Mahatma Gandhi*

Practice sharpens, but over schooling blunts the edge.
If your horse isn't doing right, the first place to look is
yourself.

~ *Joe Heim*

If you are going to teach a horse something and have a
good relationship, you don't make him learn it—you
let him learn it.

~ **Ray Hunt**

When your horse has reached his potential, leave it.
It's such a nice feeling when you and your horses are
still friends.

~ **Dr. Reiner Klimke**

My horse's feet are as swift as rolling thunder
He carries me away from all my fears
And when the world threatens to fall asunder
His mane is there to wipe away my tears.

~ **Bonnie Lewis**

There are unknown worlds of knowledge in brutes;
and whenever you mark a horse, or a dog, with a
peculiarly mild, calm, deep-seated eye, be sure he is
an Aristotle or a Kant, tranquilly speculating upon
the mysteries in man. No philosophers so thoroughly
comprehend us as dogs and horses. They see through
us at a glance. And after all, what is a horse but
a species of four-footed dumb man, in a leathern
overall, who happens to live upon oats, and toils for
his masters, half-requited or abused, like the biped
hewers of wood and drawers of water? But there is
a touch of divinity even in brutes, and a special halo
about a horse, that should forever exempt him from
indignities. As for those majestic, magisterial truck-
horses of the docks, I would as soon think of striking a
judge on the bench, as to lay violent hand upon their
holy hides.

*~ Herman Melville*

If your horse says no, you either asked the wrong
question, or asked the question wrong.

*~ Pat Parelli*

Men are better when riding, more just and more
understanding, and more alert and more at ease
and more under-taking, and better knowing of all
countries and all passages; in short and long all good
customs and manners cometh thereof, and the health
of man and of his soul.

*~ Edward Plantagenet*

A horse loves freedom, and the weariest old work
horse will roll on the ground or break into a
lumbering gallop when he is turned loose into the
open.

*~ Gerald Raferty*

A Horseman should know neither fear, nor anger.

*~ James Rarey*

You cannot train a horse with shouts and expect it to
obey a whisper.

*~ Dagobert D. Runes*

Only when you see through the eyes of the horse, can you lead the dance of the mind.

*~ Pete Spates*

Some of my best friends never say a word to me.

*~ Author Unknown*

The best teachers are those who show you where to look, but don't tell you what to see.

*~ Author Unknown*

Home is where your horse is. So I'll be in the barn.

*~ Author Unknown*

Courage is being scared to death but still saddling up anyways.

*~ Author Unknown*

To ride or not to ride? What a stupid question!

*~ Author Unknown*

A horse already knows how to be a horse; the rider
has to learn how to become a rider. A horse without
a rider is still a horse; a rider without a horse is no
longer a rider.

~ *Author Unknown*

Nothing moves me more than when on the way to
fetching my mare in the morning than the sound of
her neighing to me as I open the gate.

~ *Author Unknown*

Look back at our struggle for freedom,
Trace our present day's strength to its source;
And you'll find that man's pathway to glory
Is strewn with the bones of the horse.

~ *Author Unknown*

To err is human, to forgive, Equine.

~ *Author Unknown*

We dream of a day that humans take responsibility for
their actions, and realise horses are a privilege, not a
right.

~ *Author Unknown*

Some people think to be strong is never to feel pain.
In reality the strongest people are the ones who feel it,
understand it, and accept it!

*~ Author Unknown*

Don't interfere with something that ain't botherin' ya
none.

*~ Cowboy Wisdom*

The biggest troublemaker you'll probably ever have
to deal with watches you shave his face in the mirror
every morning.

*~ Cowboy Wisdom*

If you're ridin' ahead of the herd, take a look back
every now and then to make sure it's still there with
ya.

*~ Cowboy Wisdom*

# Giving

When people say it's just a horse,

they just don't understand.

...and the dust returns to the ground it came from,
and the spirit returns to God who gave it.

*~ Bible, Ecclesiastes 12:7*

A horse is the projection of peoples' dreams about
themselves—strong, powerful, beautiful—and it has
the capability of giving us escape from our mundane
existence.

*~ Pam Brown*

All things are possible until they are proved
impossible and even the impossible may only be so, as
of now.

*~ Pearl S. Buck*

When the storm clouds in the west
Are quickly gathering
The ponies they run wild there
Before it rains
You'll see their sleek dark bodies
Brightly gleaming
You know the fire is flying through
Their brains

*~ Jeffrey Bullock, "Ponies" (John Denver)*

One reason why birds and horses are not unhappy is because they are not trying to impress other birds and horses.

*~ Dale Carnegie*

We make a living by what we get, but we make a life by what we give.

*~ Winston Churchill*

It is the very difficult horses that have the most to give you.

~ *Lendon Gray*

Learn to see things as they really are, not as we imagine they are.

~ *Vernon Howard*

Yesterday is history. Tomorrow is a mystery. And today? Today is a gift. That's why we call it the present.

~ *Babatunde Olatunji*

There are no secrets to success. It's the result of preparation, hard work, and learning from failure.

~ *Colin Powell*

A boy is a long time before he knows his alphabet, longer before he has learned to spell, and perhaps several years before he can read distinctly; and yet there are some people who, as soon a they get on a young horse, entirely undressed and untaught, fancy that by beating and spurring they will make him a dressed horse in one morning only. I would fain ask such stupid people whether by beating a boy they would teach him to read without first showing him the alphabet? Sure they would beat him to death before they would make him read.

~ *Monty Roberts*

When your horse bolts for 10 minutes flat, you know to get off and give up. The question is, how?

~ *Annarose Robinson*

Remember, the conversation between you and your horse must never be dull or inert. It should be, "Ask, receive, give. Ask, receive, give." Ask with your body and legs; receive through your body into your hands; give primarily with the hands, but also with your body and legs, so that you can ask all over again, receive again and give again. The give is your thanks. If you don't give, you must ask harder the next time, and even harder after that, until you end up with a dead or resistant horse.

~ *Sally Swift*

Horses first. The rest later.

*~ Author Unknown*

Give a horse what he needs and he will give you his heart in return.

*~ Author Unknown*

To get respect you must give it.

*~ Author Unknown*

A good rider can hear his horse speak to him. A great rider can hear his horse whisper. But a bad rider won't hear his horse even if it screams at him!

*~ Author Unknown*

Equestrian activity teaches young ladies to cope with large, friendly, but dumb creatures—the ideal training for marriage.

*~ Author Unknown*

My horse is very quick. Sometimes he's so quick he leaves me behind.

*~ Author Unknown*

The hardest thing about learning to ride is
the ground!

*~ Author Unknown*

Anything is possible. If you just believe.

*~ Author Unknown*

Never stop asking "why?"

*~ Author Unknown*

I dare you to move. I dare you to lift yourself up
off the floor. I dare you to move like today never
happened. It's not whether you get knocked down. It's
whether you get up again.

*~ Author Unknown*

The only second chance is to make the same
mistake twice.

*~ Author Unknown*

Obstacles are really not a pain, they just make the
journey more interesting.

*~ Author Unknown*

Sometimes there is no next time, no time outs, no second chances, sometimes it's now or never.

~ *Author Unknown*

Now it's a little too late for you and your white horse to come around.

~ *Author Unknown*

It's always been and always will be the same in the world: The horse does the work and the coachman is tipped.

~ *Author Unknown*

If it don't seem like it's worth the effort, then it probably ain't.

~ *Cowboy Wisdom*

The horse will leap over trenches, will jump out of them, will do anything else, provided one grants him praise and respite after his accomplishment.

~ *Xenophon*

# Healing

Horses
aren't my
whole life...
They make
my life
whole

The future has been losing the wisdom of the past ever since the freeway bypassed the corral....Damn!

### ~ *Ken Alstad*

If you come to a fork in the road, take it.

### ~ *Yogi Berra*

Your horse is a mirror to your soul. Sometimes you might not like what your see and sometimes you will.

### ~ *Buck Brannaman*

If the world were truly a rational place, men would
ride sidesaddle.

~ *Rita Mae Brown*

Our greatest glory is not in never falling, but in rising
every time we fall.

~ *Confucius*

A canter is the cure for every evil.

~ *Benjamin Disraeli*

A good horse makes short miles.

~ *George Eliot*

It is easier to get an actor to be a cowboy than to get a
cowboy to be an actor.

~ *John Ford*

You've got to get up every morning with
determination to be able to go to bed
with satisfaction.

*~ George Lorimer*

One man's wrong lead is another man's counter canter.

*~ S.D. Price*

An onion can make people cry but there's never been a
vegetable that can make people laugh.

*~ Will Rogers*

We all fall or get taken down but what matters isn't
how we frown or even if we are found; that doesn't
make us what we are. What does make you, you is
how you pull yourself up after you've had that fall.

*~ Author Unknown*

There is no telling how many miles you will run to
chase a dream.

*~ Author Unknown*

My therapist lives in a barn.

*~ Author Unknown*

When life gets you down; ride it out.

*~ Author Unknown*

Horses are not our whole lives, but they make our lives whole.

*~ Author Unknown*

Don't ask God to make life easier, ask him to make you a stronger person.

*~ Author Unknown*

By saving horses, I lost my mind but found my soul.

*~ Author Unknown*

All I pay my psychiatrist is the cost of feed and hay, and he'll listen to me any day.

*~ Author Unknown*

Looking back now on better days, I realize I didn't do all the things I said I would but all the things I said I wouldn't.

*~ Author Unknown*

Your best friend listens to you when you don't make sense; stands by you when people call you things; argues when you're not right at all; trusts you when she knows you'll mess up; when you cry she's there helping you out and that's how I know she's truly my best friend.

*~ Author Unknown*

If you hide, I'll seek for you. If you're lost, I'll search for you. If you leave, I'll wait for you. If they try to take you away from me, I'll fight for you. Cause I never want to lose someone I love.

*~ Author Unknown*

The joy of horses is not the riding, jumping, racing, showing, or grooming, but of owning!!!

*~ Author Unknown*

Been There...Jumped That!

*~ Author Unknown*

A western horse has guts and commitment, an English horse has grace and elegance, but my horse has it all!

*~ Author Unknown*

I dream of a world where a chicken can cross the road
without having their motives questions.

*~ Author Unknown*

Saving one horse will not change the world…But
surely it would change the world for that one horse.

*~ Author Unknown*

Life is hard; it's harder if you're stupid.

*~ John Wayne*

The only good reason to ride a bull is to meet a nurse.

*~ Cowboy Wisdom*

You can't tell a horse's gait till she's broke.

*~ Cowboy Wisdom*

Behind every successful rancher is a wife who works in town.

~ *Cowgirl Wisdom*

# Kindness

"Let a horse whisper in your ear and breathe on your heart.
You will never regret it."

Frustration begins where knowledge ends.

~ *Clinton Anderson*

A horse is the projection of peoples' dreams about themselves—strong, powerful, beautiful—and it has the capability of giving us escape from our mundane existence.

~ *Pam Brown*

The horses paw and prance and neigh,
Fillies and colts like kittens play,
And dance and toss their rippled manes
Shining and soft as silken skeins;...

~ *Oliver Wendell Holmes*

I can make a General in five minutes but a good horse
is hard to replace.

~ *Abraham Lincoln*

There are only two emotions that belong in the saddle;
one is a sense of humor and the other is patience.

~ *John Lyons*

Preserve his natural gaits. Preserve his personality.
Preserve his instinct to go forward. Do this and you
must be successful because you are respecting nature's
wisdom.

~ *Franz Mairinger*

A horse will never tire of a rider who possesses both
tact and sensitivity because he will never be pushed
beyond his possibilities.

~ *Nuno Oliveira*

Poll Flexion is not Pull Flexion.

*~ Dr. Thomas Ritter*

You cannot train a horse with shouts and expect it to obey a whisper.

*~ Dagobert D. Runes*

Increased body awareness gives you a greater awareness of your inner self as well as your surroundings. Changing your habits will cultivate an ability to make clearer choices: A balanced body permits a balanced state of mind.

*~ Sally Swift*

Horse sense, n.: Stable thinking.

*~ Author Unknown*

If I smell like peppermints, I was feeding my horse treats. If I smell like shampoo, I was giving my horse a bath. If I smell like manure, I tripped.

*~ Author Unknown*

Throw your heart over the jump and your horse will follow.

*~ Author Unknown*

Unless you hear it straight from the horse's mouth... don't listen to the jackass.

*~ Author Unknown*

I'm so busy I don't know if I found a rope or lost my horse.

*~ Author Unknown*

The only stock I own has four legs.

*~ Author Unknown*

If I had a horse, I'd ride off in the sunset, where dreams, and shadows lie. To a life, where pain and sorrow don't exist, and to where hopes, and dreams become reality.

*~ Author Unknown*

Horses change lives. They give our young people confidence and self-esteem. They provide peace and tranquility to troubled souls—they give us hope!

*~ Author Unknown*

No ride is ever the last one. No horse is ever the last one you will have. Somehow there will always be other horses, other places to ride them.

*~ Author Unknown*

Your horse can only be as brave as you are.

*~ Author Unknown*

Tell me it can't be done, and I will do it.
Tell me the goal is too high, and I will reach it.
Place an obstacle in front of me. And I will soar over it. Challenge me, Dare me, or even defy me.
But do NOT underestimate me. For on the back of my horse ANYTHING is possible.

*~ Author Unknown*

Never give up on someone you can't go a day without thinking about.

*~ Author Unknown*

The greatest treasures in life are invisible to the eye but felt by the heart.

*~ Author Unknown*

You can tell a true cowboy by the type of horse that he rides.

*~ Author Unknown*

We can't all be heroes because someone has to sit on
the curb and clap as they go by.

*~ Author Unknown*

Talk low, talk slow, and don't say too much.

*~ John Wayne*

It's the horse that makes the cowboy.

*~ Cowboy Wisdom*

Cowgirls are like barbed wire...handle with care.

*~ Cowgirl Wisdom*

If anybody expects to calm a horse down by tiring
him out riding swiftly and far, his supposition is the
reverse of the truth.

*~ Xenophon*

Anything forced and misunderstood can never
be beautiful.

~ *Xenophon*

# Laughter

Having a jealous wife means if you come home with a hair on your coat, you'd better have the horse to match.

~ *Ken Alstad*

It's a lot like nuts and bolts—if the rider's nuts, the horse bolts!

~ *Nicholas Evans*

Horse sense is the thing a horse has which keeps it from betting on people.

~ *W.C. Fields*

I prefer a bike to a horse. The brakes are
more easily checked.

~ *Lambert Jeffries*

People on horses look better than they are.  People in
cars look worse than they are.

~ *Marya Mannes*

When you're young and you fall off a horse, you may
break something. When you're my age and you fall
off, you splatter.

~ *Roy Rogers*

You know horses are smarter than people. You never
heard of a horse going broke betting on people.

~ *Will Rogers*

Whoever said a horse was dumb, was dumb.

~ *Will Rogers*

The quickest way to double your money is to fold it over and put it back into your pocket.

~ *Will Rogers*

There are three kinds of men: The ones that learn by reading. The few who learn by observation. The rest of them have to pee on the electric fence.

~ *Will Rogers*

Some of my best leading men have been dogs and horses.

~ *Elizabeth Taylor*

There are only two emotions that belong in the saddle; one is a sense of humor and the other is patience.

~ *Author Unknown*

The good thing about talkin' to your horse is he don't talk back.

~ *Author Unknown*

Who needs men when you have a horse?
Oh...wait...someone's gotta do the paying!

~ *Author Unknown*

Old cowboys never die, they just smell that way.

~ *Author Unknown*

A woman needs two animals—the horse of her dreams
and a jackass to pay for it.

~ *Author Unknown*

When you ask for free advice, you get what
you paid for.

~ *Author Unknown*

Genius has its limits. Stupidity knows no bounds.

~ *Author Unknown*

There is a fine line between fishing and standing on
the shore like an idiot.

~ *Author Unknown*

Ridin' a bronc is like dancin' with a girl.  The trick is
matchin' yer partner's rhythm.

*~ Cowboy Wisdom*


Cowboy dress is determined by three factors: weather,
work, and vanity.

*~ Cowboy Wisdom*


A bronc rider should be light in the head and
heavy in the seat.

*~ Cowboy Wisdom*


It takes a big man to cry... but it takes a bigger man
to laugh at that man.

*~ Cowboy Wisdom*


Some men talk 'cause they got somethin' to say.
Others talk 'cause they got to say somethin'.

*~ Cowboy Wisdom*


Broke is what happens when a cowboy lets his
yearnin's get ahead of his earnin's.

*~ Cowboy Wisdom*

It takes fewer muscles to smile than to frown... and
fewer still to ignore someone completely.

~ *Cowboy Wisdom*

An old timer's a man who's had a lot of interesting
experiences—some of 'em true.

~ *Cowboy Wisdom*

There's two theories to arguin' with a woman.
Neither one works.

~ *Cowboy Wisdom*

It don't take no genius to spot a goat in a
flock of sheep.

~ *Cowboy Wisdom*

Tellin' a man to git lost and makin' him do it are two
entirely different propositions.

~ *Cowboy Wisdom*

Never ask a man the size of his spread.

~ *Cowboy Wisdom*

# *Love*

COWGIRL WISDOM:
When playing hard to get,
it's better to have
a fast horse

If a man works like a horse for his money, there are a lot of girls anxious to take him down the bridal path.

~ *Marty Allen*

The daughter who won't lift a finger in the house is the same child who cycles madly off in the pouring rain to spend all morning mucking out a stable.

~ *Samantha Armstrong*

Somewhere in time's own space, there must be some
sweet pastured place Where creeks sing on and tall
trees grow, some paradise where the horses go;
For, by the love that guides my pen, I know great
horses live again.

~ *Stanley Harrison*

To many, the words love, hope, and dreams are
synonymous with horses.

~ *Oliver Wendell Holmes*

My horse's feet are as swift as rolling thunder
He carries me away from all my fears
And when the world threatens to fall asunder
His mane is there to wipe away my tears.

~ *Bonnie Lewis*

Love means attention, which means looking after the
things we love. We call this stable management.

~ *George H. Morris*

A Hibernian sage once wrote that there are three
things a man never forgets: The girl of his early
youth, a devoted teacher, and a great horse.

### ~C.J.J. Mullen

He knows when you're happy
He knows when you're comfortable
He knows when you're confident
And he *always* knows when you have carrots.

### ~ Author Unknown

By loving and understanding animals, perhaps we
humans shall come to understand each other.

### ~ Author Unknown

When your horse follows you without being asked,
when he rubs his head on yours, and when you look at
him and feel a tingle down your spine you know you
are loved...do you love him back?

### ~ Author Unknown

Horses—if God made anything more beautiful, he
kept it for himself.

### ~ Author Unknown

All horses deserve, at least once in their lives, to be loved by a little girl.

*~ Author Unknown*

A true horse person is someone who not just loves to ride, but LIVES to ride.

*~ Author Unknown*

Whoever said diamonds are a girl's best friend...never owned a horse.

*~ Author Unknown*

Let a horse whisper in your ear and breathe on your heart because you will never regret it.

*~ Author Unknown*

Before responding to party invitations...I check the show schedule.

*~ Author Unknown*

Trust in God, but tie your horse.

*~ Author Unknown*

Because no one will ever understand your love for that
horse smell or the peace it brings your soul...
breathe deep.

*~ Author Unknown*

People come and go but horses leave hoof prints on
your heart.

*~ Author Unknown*

When people say it's JUST a horse, they
JUST don't understand.

*~ Author Unknown*

You can take a horse out of the wild, but you can't
take the wild out of the horse!

*~ Author Unknown*

He may knock down a pole, but he will never break
my heart.

*~ Author Unknown*

A barn isn't a barn if there are no horses in it.

*~ Author Unknown*

My barn is my happy place.

*~ Author Unknown*

Horses are like potato chips, you can't just have one.

*~ Author Unknown*

A horse will cross any bridge you build as long as the first one is from him to you.

*~ Author Unknown*

Horse people are a different breed.

*~ Author Unknown*

When we love an animal as our family, we begin to understand animals are our family.

*~ Anthony Douglas Williams*

When playing hard to get, it's better to have a fast horse.

*~ Cowgirl Wisdom*

Every cowgirl knows...if you're wantin' to find yourself a good stallion don't go looking in the donkey corral.

*~ Cowgirl Wisdom*

Don't flatter yourself cowboy; I was looking at
your horse.

~ *Cowgirl Wisdom*

# Respect

Always remember that your present situation is not your final destination. The best is yet to come.

Always remember that the future comes one day
at a time.

~ *Dean Acheson*

Always remember that you are absolutely unique. Just
like everyone else.

~ *Margaret Mead*

Always remember: You're braver than you believe, and
stronger than you seem, and smarter than you think.

~ *A.A. Milne*

Always remember to smile and look up at what
you got in life.

~ *Marilyn Monroe*

Always remember a man that straddles a fence usually
has a sore crotch.

~ *Author Unknown*

Always remember a change of pastures makes fer a
fatter calf.

~ *Author Unknown*

Always remember our money don't last as long as a
rattler in a cowboy's boot.

~ *Author Unknown*

Always remember a lot of folks would do more prayin'
could they find a soft spot fer their knees.

~ *Author Unknown*

Always remember there's only two things I'm afeared
of, a decent woman an' bein' left afoot.

~ *Author Unknown*

Always remember yuh can't turn a woman mor'n yuh
can a runaway hog.

~ *Author Unknown*

Always remember a grass widdow is a dangerous
critter fer a bachelor cowboy.

~ *Author Unknown*

Always remember if the Lord had intended us to fight
like a dog, He'd given us longer claws an' teeth.

~ *Author Unknown*

Always remember if the saddle creaks, it's not paid fer.

~ *Author Unknown*

Always remember the bigger the mouth the better
it looks shut.

~ *Author Unknown*

Always remember likker will make yuh see double an'
feel single.

~ *Author Unknown*

Always remember don't never interfere with nothin'
what don't bother yuh none.

~ *Author Unknown*

Always remember the Lord done put tumbleweeds here to show which way the wind is blowin'.

*~ Author Unknown*

Always remember most men are like a bob-wire fence, they have their good points.

*~ Author Unknown*

Always remember to forget the things that made you sad, but never forget to remember the things that made you glad.

*~ Author Unknown*

Always remember that your present situation is not your final destination. The best is yet to come.

*~ Author Unknown*

Always remember to be kind, be fair, be honest, and be true, as all of these things will come back to you.

*~ Author Unknown*

Always remember to slow down in life; live, breathe, and learn; take a look around you whenever you have time and never forget everything and every person that has the least place within your heart.

*~ Author Unknown*

Always remember to say "thank you."

~ *Author Unknown*

Always remember God will never take anything away from you without the intention of replacing it with something much better.

~ *Author Unknown*

Always remember a friend will stick with you 'til they're cuttin' ice in Death Valley.

~ *Cowboy Wisdom*

Always remember cussin' a range cook is as risky as brandin' a mule's tail.

~ *Cowboy Wisdom*

Always remember yer not overweight—just a foot too short.

~ *Cowboy Wisdom*

Always remember a man that looks over his shoulder
at every piece of straight road ain't been livin' a
straight life.

~ *Cowboy Wisdom*

Always remember that crossin' a woman is 'bout as
dangerous as walkin' in quicksand over hell.

~ *Cowboy Wisdom*

Always remember boothill is full of fellers that pulled
their triggers without aiming.

~ *Cowboy Wisdom*

# Rewarding

A horse is
the projection
of peoples' dreams
about themselves...
Strong
Powerful
Beautiful

Courage is fear that has said its prayers.

~ *Karl Barth*

Of all creatures God made at the Creation, there is none more excellent, or so much to be respected as a Horse.

~ *Bedouin Legend*

Be wary of the horse with a sense of humor.

~ *Pam Brown*

You must in all Airs follow the strength, spirit, and
disposition of the horse, and do nothing against
nature; for art is but to set nature in order, and
nothing else.

~ *William Cavendish*

There is something about the outside of a horse that is
good for the inside of a man.

~ *Winston Churchill*

The most beautiful, the most spirited and the most
inspiring creature ever to print foot on the grasses
of America.

~ *J. Frank Dobie*

True cowboys are the ones who aren't afraid
to get dirty.

~ *Lane Frost*

I heard a neigh. Oh, such a brisk and melodious neigh as that was! My very heart leaped with delight at the sound.

*~ Nathaniel Hawthorne*

It excites me that no matter how much machinery replaces the horse, the work it can do is still measured in horsepower...even in this space age. And although a riding horse often weighs half a ton, and a big drafter a full ton, either can be led about by a piece of string if he has been wisely trained. This to me is a constant source of wonder, and challenge.

*~ Marguerite Henry*

Four things greater than all things are—women and horses and power and war.

*~ Rudyard Kipling*

She knew that the horse, born to serve nobly, had waited in vain for someone noble to serve.

*~ D.H. Lawrence*

Honor lies in the mane of a horse.

~ *Herman Melville*

There is a touch of divinity even in brutes, and a special halo about a horse, that should forever exempt him from indignities.

~ *Herman Melville*

A horse! A horse! My kingdom for a horse!

~ *William Shakespeare*

A man on a horse is spiritually as well as physically bigger than a man on foot.

~ *John Steinbeck*

There is no secret so close as that between a rider and his horse.

~ *R. S. Surtees*

Coffee, Chocolate, Cowboys...some things are just better rich.

~ *Author Unknown*

Feeling down? Saddle up.

~ *Author Unknown*

A horse is poetry in motion.

~ *Author Unknown*

Life is a Rodeo; take it as you get it.

~ *Author Unknown*

Risk everything, fear nothing, have no regrets.

~ *Author Unknown*

Ask not what your horse can do for you—ask what you can do for your horse.

~ *Author Unknown*

Wild oats aren't meant for sowing—but they make a nice trail snack.

~ *Author Unknown*

When to see a horse you think low intelligence, to see a man high intelligence, but to mix to make a friendship you seem to get greater intelligence.

*~ Author Unknown*

Jumping is just dressage with speed bumps!

*~ Author Unknown*

Whoever said that money cannot buy happiness didn't know where to buy a horse.

*~ Author Unknown*

Riding is not a sport, it is a passion. If you do not share the passion, you do not know the sport, and therefore are wasting your time.

*~ Author Unknown*

A horse is like a violin, first it must be tuned, and when tuned it must be accurately played.

*~Author Unknown*

Bread may feed my body, but my horse feeds my soul.

*~ Author Unknown*

Make time for your loved ones. We are not promised tomorrow so make the most of today.

*~ Author Unknown*

Every time you ride, you're either teaching or un-teaching your horse.

*~ Gordon Wright*

# Understanding

Advice from a HORSE
Take life's hurdles in stride.
Loosen the reins.
Be free spirited.
Keep the burrs
from under your saddle.
Carry your friends
when they need it.
Keep stable.
Gallop to greatness!
—Ilan Shamir

**Being Irritated:** Now don't go and get a burr under your saddle.

**Being Unique:** Horse people are a different breed.

**Beware:** I ride horses, which means I own pitchforks, have the strength to haul hay, and have the guts to scream at a half-ton animal after being kicked…you will not be a problem.

**Commitment:** Wild horses couldn't drag him away.

**Eagerness:** Chomping at the bit to go.

**Full of Mischief:** On the back of his white horse.

**Gambling:** Play the ponies.

**Hindsight:** It's always easy to remember that you should have closed the barn door after the horses have gotten out.

**Health:** The best color of a horse is fat.

**Humility:** Get off your high horse.

**Hunger:** I could eat a horse.

**Impatience:** Hold your horses.

**Knowledge:** You've got to control yourself before you kin control your horse.

**Know Your Limits:** Don't beat a dead horse.

**Not Being Direct:** You're takin' the long way around the barn.

**Notice:** If my horse doesn't like you I probably won't either

**Not the End of the World:** This is not the death of the little horse.

**Not Thinking:** Looks like you've put the cart before the horse.

**Old Age:** Long in the tooth.

**Patience:** Hold your horses!

**Pride: Pride rides a horse and walks back.**

**Priorities:** Don't change horses midstream.

**Quitting:** Stop horsing around.

**Retirement:** Put a horse out to pasture.

**Small Town:** This is a one-horse town.

**Strength:** Strong as a horse.

**Taking Advantage:** Everyone lays a burden on the willing horse.

**Truth:** Straight from the horse's mouth.

**Unexpected Success:** A dark horse.

**Word to the Wise:** A nod is as good as a wink to a blind horse.

# Uplifting

the wind from *heaven* which blows between a horse's ears

The horse is God's gift to mankind.

*~ Arabian Proverb*

My treasures do not clink together or glitter;
They gleam in the sun and neigh in the night.

*~ Arabian Proverb*

The wind of heaven is that which blows between a
horse's ears.

*~ Arabian Proverb*

Judge not the horse by his saddle.

*~ Chinese Proverb*

You think you lost your horse?
Who knows, he may bring a whole herd back
to you someday.

*~ Chinese Proverb*

Care, and not fine stables, makes a good horse.

*~ Danish Proverb*

One cannot shoe a running horse.

*~ Dutch Proverb*

If wishes were horses, beggars would ride.

*~ English Proverb*

Look not a gift horse in the mouth.

*~ English Proverb*

You can take a horse to water but you can't make it
drink.

*~ English Proverb*

Where there's a will there's a way.

*~ English Proverb*

Misfortunes come on horseback and depart on foot.

*~ French Proverb*

A colt is worth little if it does not break its halter.

*~ French Proverb*

What the colt learns in youth he continues in old age.

*~ French Proverb*

It's too late to close the stable door after the
horse has bolted.

*~ French Proverb*

A colt you may break, but an old horse you never can.

*~ French Proverb*

Set a beggar on horseback, and he'll out ride the Devil.

~ *German Proverb*

Sell the cow, buy the sheep, but never be without the horse.

~ *Irish Proverb*

It is the good horse that draws its own cart.

~ *Irish Proverb*

Youth sheds many a skin. The steed does not retain its speed forever.

~ *Irish Proverb*

Trouble rides a fast horse.

~ *Italian Proverb*

It is not enough for a man to learn how to ride; he must learn how to fall.

~ *Mexican Proverb*

We will be known forever by the tracks we leave behind.

~ *Native American Proverb*

When in doubt, let your horse do the thinkin'.

~ *Old West Proverb*

Worry is like a rockin' horse. It's something to do that don't get you nowhere.

~ *Old West Proverb*

No one sees a fly on a trotting horse.

~ *Polish Proverb*

The man who does not love a horse cannot
love a woman.

~ *Spanish Proverb*

A horse is worth more than riches.

~ *Spanish Proverb*

In buying a horse or taking a wife, shut your eyes
tight and commend yourself to God.

~ *Tuscan Proverb*

Have a horse of your own and then you may borrow
another's.

~ *Welsh Proverb*

The wagon rests in winter, the sleigh in summer, the
horse never.

~ *Yiddish Proverb*

# Appendices
## When I Count My Blessings...

# Appendix: Favorite Quotes

Quote: _____
_____
_____

Quote: _____
_____
_____

Quote: _____
_____
_____

Quote: _____
_____
_____

Quote: _____
_____
_____

Quote: _____
_____
_____

Quote: _____
_____
_____

# Appendix: Horse Checklist

## Accomplishments
Horses …

_____
_____
_____
_____
_____
_____
_____
_____
_____
_____

## Caring
Horses …

_____
_____
_____
_____
_____
_____
_____
_____
_____
_____

## Favorites
Horses ...

_____

_____

_____

_____

_____

_____

_____

_____

_____

_____

## Friendships
Horses ...

_____

_____

_____

_____

_____

_____

_____

_____

_____

## Healing
Horses ...

_____

_____

_____

_____

_____

_____

_____

_____

_____

## Lessons
Horses ...

_____

_____

_____

_____

_____

_____

_____

_____

_____

## Little Things
Horses ...

_____
_____
_____
_____
_____
_____
_____
_____
_____
_____

## Memories
Horses ...

_____
_____
_____
_____
_____
_____
_____
_____
_____

## Riding

Horses ...

_____

_____

_____

_____

_____

_____

_____

_____

_____

## Significant Moments

Horses ...

_____

_____

_____

_____

_____

_____

_____

_____

## Things I Never Expected
Horses …

_____

_____

_____

_____

_____

_____

_____

_____

_____

_____

## Other
Horses …

_____

_____

_____

_____

_____

_____

_____

_____

_____

# Appendix: Horse Journal

January: _____

_____

_____

_____

_____

_____

_____

_____

_____

_____

February: _____

_____

_____

_____

_____

_____

_____

_____

_____

_____

March: _____

_____

_____

_____

_____

_____

_____

_____

_____

_____

_____

April: _____

_____

_____

_____

_____

_____

_____

_____

_____

_____

May: _____

_____

_____

_____

_____

_____

_____

_____

_____

_____

_____

June: _____

_____

_____

_____

_____

_____

_____

_____

_____

_____

_____

July: _____

_____

_____

_____

_____

_____

_____

_____

_____

_____

August: _____

_____

_____

_____

_____

_____

_____

_____

_____

_____

September: _____

_____

_____

_____

_____

_____

_____

_____

_____

_____

_____

October: _____

_____

_____

_____

_____

_____

_____

_____

_____

_____

_____

November: _____

_____

_____

_____

_____

_____

_____

_____

_____

_____

_____

December:_____

_____

_____

_____

_____

_____

_____

_____

_____

_____

# Index

# About the Editors

**Gina Pecho** was raised in Orland Park, IL and enjoyed living in the Chicago Suburbs most of her life. It wasn't until she met her husband, Tony Pecho, that this city girl fell in love with a country boy and the country life along with it. Since adapting to life in a rural area, Gina has developed a strong passion for animals.

Being a part of the Illinois Horse Rescue of Will County, she welcomes the opportunity to spend time with the many types of animals the rescue takes in. Being especially fond of holding and feeding the tiniest of animals, Gina specializes in the care of small, orphaned animals. In addition to nurturing motherless baby animals, Gina is also the Administrator for the rescue and manages many of the essential details to keep the office running smoothly. Every animal she comes in contact with has touched her heart in some way.

**Jessica Pecho** has spent her entire life loving and caring for all kinds of animals. She works for Illinois Horse Rescue of Will County as the Barn Director. She knows every rescue animal that has ever been there or is there now. She instructs and teaches the volunteers about the many rescues. The best part of her job is to find forever homes for the wonderful rescues in her care.

**Illinois Horse Rescue of Will County** was founded to provide shelter and care for mistreated or abandoned horses. They provide shelter, food, and veterinary services for these animals until a suitable home can be found. As secondary services, they also provide educational and therapeutic programs to local schools and charities with and about these animals.

Illinois Horse Rescue of Will County strives to represent both horse and human interests by creating a forum that promotes personal growth through equine interaction and care, as well as learning and rehabilitation. This unique forum supports an environment of unconditional love and companionship in which rescued horses and people can work together towards healing each other. Both humans and horses gain a solid purpose, thereby strengthening their ability to be a positive force in the lives of others and of themselves.

Illinois Horse Rescue of Will County is a 501(c)(3) non-profit organization with offices and barn facilities in Beecher, IL and Peotone, IL. Their experience and dedication has earned them a reputation for honesty, compassion, and responsibility.

For more information please visit: www.illinoishorserescue.org

Illinois Horse Rescue
OF WILL COUNTY

## Your Donation Makes a Difference

Illinois Horse Rescue of Will County was founded to provide shelter and care for mistreated or abandoned horses. We provide shelter, food, and veterinary services for these animals until a suitable home can be found. As secondary services, we provide educational and therapeutic programs to local schools and charities with and about these animals.

- Your contribution is used to buy food, medicine, and veterinary care.
- Animal Rescue and Safety is what we do every day.
- We're a 501(c)(3) non-profit, so your donation is tax-deductible.
- We believe every animal deserves a second chance, and no one is turned away.
- You can give in confidence; we are a GuideStar Approved Charity.

Please contact us directly to make a donation or to purchase additional copies of *The Little Book of Horse Quotes.*

***Illinois Horse Rescue of Will County***
P.O. Box 1019
Peotone, IL 60468

**Phone:** (708) 258-3959
**Email:** office@illinoishorserescue.org
**Web site:** www.illinoishorserescue.org

DONATE NOW

Help us save more lives

### YES! I want to help the rescue horses at *Illinois Horse Rescue of Will County*

Name _____
Address_____
_____
City _____ State_____
ZIP _____

Please enter my donation now. Here is my gift.
[ ] **$15.00**
[ ] **$25.00**
[ ] **Other** _____
**Check enclosed [ ]**
*Please make check payable to Illinois Horse Rescue of Will County and send to:*
*Illinois Horse Rescue of Will County*
P.O. Box 1019
Peotone, IL 60468
**Charge my credit card VISA [ ] MC [ ]**
**Card number**_____
**Expires**_____
**Signature**_____
**Name** _____
**Address**_____
_____
City _____ State_____
ZIP _____

Made in the USA
Lexington, KY
19 December 2014